MASTER VOCAB TERMINOLOGY

BUSINESS ENGLISH IN USE

ESSENTIAL BUSINESS TERMS, WORDING & IDIOMS FOR WORK MEETINGS, BUSINESS PLANS, CONTRACTS, REPORTS, PROPOSALS, MARKETING, FINANCE & INVESTMENT

BUSINESS ENGLISH ORIGINALS SERIES

Copyright © 2022 by Marc Roche. All Right Reserved.

An earlier, more basic version of this book was originally published as *Business English Vocabulary: Advanced Masterclass* in 2018. No part of this business vocabulary book may be reproduced, distributed, or transmitted in any form or by any means, including photocopying, recording, or other electronic or mechanical methods, or by any information storage and retrieval system without the prior written permission of the publisher, except in the case of very brief quotations embodied in critical reviews and certain other noncommercial uses permitted by copyright law.

Contents

About The Author	10
Other Business English Books in This Series by Marc Roche	11
Contributors & Influencers	15
FREE COMPANION EBOOK: "Common Investment Terms Explained"	16
ABOUT THIS BUSINESS ENGLISH VOCABULARY BOOK.	18
How to Use This Book	20
CHAPTER 1. CORE BUSINESS CONCEPTS	21
'Value' in Business	22
'Testing' Products & Services	23
A Niche	24
Demographics & Customer Data	24
Target Customers & Target Market	25
Competition	25
Competitor Analysis	26
Revenue	26
Assets	27
Net Profit	27
Gross Profit	28
Break-Even Point	28
Cash flow	29
Fixed Costs	29

Profit Margin	30
Overheads	30
Stakeholders	31
Chapter Review Exercise	32
CHAPTER 2. PRODUCTION CYCLES & PROCESSES	**42**
Describing Sequences	43
Vocabulary Exercises	44
CHAPTER 3. LINE GRAPH VOCABULARY	**51**
Vocabulary Exercises	52
Expressions for Line Graphs	63
Structures for Summarising Change	65
Adding Transitions to Your Sentences	69
While/Whereas/Although/Though	70
Comparing and Contrasting Similar Data	71
CHAPTER 4. BAR CHART VOCABULARY	**72**
CHAPTER 5. NUMBERS, PERCENTAGES & FRACTIONS	**76**
Expressing Approximations	77
Percentages & Fractions	82
CHAPTER 6. PUBLIC SPEAKING & TRAINING	**85**
Language for Teaching & Presenting	86
Meetings & Discussions	93
CHAPTER 7. COMMONLY CONFUSED WORDS	**101**
CHAPTER 8. COMMON CORPORATE TERMS	**108**
KPI (Key Performance Indicator):	109

Customer Acquisition Cost	109
Customer Lifetime Value	109
Customer Satisfaction Score	109
Sales Target % (Forecast/Actual)	110
Revenue per Customer	110
ROA (Return on Assets)	110
Current Ratio (Assets/Liabilities)	110
Employee experience	111
Employee engagement	111
Employee satisfaction	111
Psychological safety	111
Consolidation Exercise	112
Talent management	117
Change management	117
Learning & Development (L&D)	117
Growth mindset	117
Retention	118
Staff (employee) turnover	118
Core values	118
Company mission	118
Company vision	118
Company culture	119
Culture fit	119
Diversity & Inclusion (D&I)	119

Performance management	119
Ad-hoc	120
Sync up	120
Employee check-in	120
Performance review	120
360 feedback	120
Objectives and Key Results (OKRs)	121
Employee appreciation	121
Consolidation Exercise	122
CHAPTER 9. PROFESSIONAL VERBS & PHRASAL VERBS WITH PRACTICE EXERCISES	**130**
Abide by	131
Accede to	131
Account for	131
Account to	132
Adhere to	132
Amount to	132
Appertain to (or pertain to)	133
Exercise 1	**133**
Break down	135
Break off	135
Break up	135
Exercise 2	**136**
Enter into	137

Entitle to (Adj. Entitled to)	137
Exclude	137
Exercise 3	138
Factor in	139
Find in favour of/Against (also: Rule in favour of/against)	139
Exercise 4	139
Hand Down	140
Exercise 5	141
Pass off	142
Provide that	142
Exercise 6	143
Set forth	144
Strike Out	144
Sum Up	144
Weigh up	145
Exercise 7	145
Answers	147
CHAPTER 10. MASTER BUSINESS IDIOMS & BUSINESS JARGON	152
112 BUSINESS IDIOMS & COMMON TERMS WITH BETTER OPTIONS	157
A	157
B	161
C	167

D	170
E	175
F	177
G	179
H	183
I	184
J	185
K	186
L	187
M	190
N	193
O	194
P	197
R	200
S	204
T	209
U	213
V	213
W	214
Z	214
BONUS CHAPTER 11. FREE BOOK: FINANCE & INVESTMENT TERMS EXPLAINED	216
The End & Special Thank You	221

About The Author

Marc has been a business writing & legal English coach and an academic English exam prep specialist for over ten years. He has collaborated with organizations such as the British Council, the Royal Melbourne Institute of Technology (RMIT), the University of Technology Sydney, and multinationals like Nike, GlaxoSmithKline, and Bolsas y Mercados, among others.

OTHER BUSINESS ENGLISH BOOKS IN THIS SERIES BY MARC ROCHE

<u>Business English Writing: Advanced Masterclass by Marc Roche</u>

Business Email: Write to Win

by Marc Roche

Email Writing: Advanced by Marc Roche

Business Writing Skills Workbook: Master Business Grammar, Punctuation & Style by Marc Roche

Contributors & Influencers

Amazon Associate Links

Word Power Made Easy by Norman Lewis

HBR Guide to Better Business Writing by Bryan A. Garner

The Vocabulary Builder Workbook by Chris Lele

The Well-Spoken Thesaurus by Tom Heehler

Business Vocabulary in Use by Bill Mascull

FREE COMPANION EBOOK:

"COMMON INVESTMENT TERMS EXPLAINED"

Sign up to the FREE VIP List today to grab your FREE downloadable eBook ☺

Details can be found at the end of the book.

-blank page-

ABOUT THIS BUSINESS ENGLISH VOCABULARY BOOK.

Business vocabulary is essential to speak about, write about, and understand business concepts. However, it is also the key that will allow you to research business-related topics and gain more in-depth knowledge about finance, strategy, economics, and many other areas.

Gaining an understanding of key business vocabulary also vastly improves your writing and conversation skills and your ability to listen with intent.

Master Business Vocabulary & Terminology: Business English in Use is a Master Vocabulary Builder for Advanced Business English Speaking & Writing. This book is full of business English vocabulary, including specialized exercises and explanations.

Master Business Vocabulary & Terminology: Business English in Use is ideal for anyone who has problems understanding, remembering, and using business

English vocabulary and for anyone who wants to speak better business English with fluency and confidence. Don't waste hours researching words and trying to understand their meaning. This book will make your learning more efficient.

How to Use This Book

This business English vocabulary and terminology book is specifically designed to provide students with a solid foundation in the general concepts and terminology of business. While it is not an exhaustive course, it provides highly effective training in the general business vocabulary that every professional must understand. It also goes beyond vocabulary training by teaching the concepts and background knowledge needed to fully understand and discuss the terms being used.

The topics covered in this book include marketing, strategy, accounting, finance, investment, emails, and meetings, among others.

CHAPTER 1. CORE BUSINESS CONCEPTS

This chapter will look at some core business concepts that will help you expand your vocabulary and business knowledge further throughout the rest of the book.

Don't worry; you can always return to this section later if you need to review anything.

Let's get started!

'Value' in Business

Ask yourself about your company's core values and what purpose the business serves. How does it 'bring value' to people? Providing value should arguably be at the core of any business or organization.

- Does the business aim to reduce the shortage of high-quality daycare centers in their community?
- Does it provide a place for customers to enjoy locally-made pasta dishes?
- Does it offer reasonably priced, high-quality produce straight from local organic farms?

Knowing the purpose of the business will ensure that you have a compass for the decisions you will make in the future.

It also provides an excellent starting point for meetings, negotiations, business plans, and emails.

'Testing' Products & Services

Whether it is a service or product, you need to at least **test** your idea before **launching**. This is like creating a prototype before you start selling anything.

Maybe you or your company wants to open a new café, but you test the response to your coffee in the area by providing it to local shoppers or friends and family and then record their opinions.

Talking with others and putting the idea out there will help you know the market, who will buy, and who competes in that market (the **competition**).

You can even **test** your product or service by creating social media and website profiles, combining them with social media ads, and **testing** and **measuring** the response against your **target market** (the type of customer you want to serve).

Gary Vaynerchuk advocates this technique as it saves you a lot of time and money, and it stops you from wasting your precious time creating products that no one will buy.

This is about constructive criticism. You may want to open a coffee shop, but after talking to an expert or potential customer, your idea may evolve, and you may come up with a better concept that serves a particular **'niche.'**

A Niche

A **niche** is a specific group of people who like a certain thing, or in other words, a specific section of the market.

Demographics & Customer Data

Any relevant information relating to your customers and their region is classed as demographics. Age, gender, level of education, income, interests, race, ethnicity/ cultural background, religion, marital status, etc.

Target Customers & Target Market

Your **target customer** is the specific section of the market (or **niche**) who would be interested in your product or service. The general recommendation here is to be as specific as possible when deciding who they are.

- What are the **demographics** of your customers or clients?
- You should ensure that you know the area your business serves, who lives there, and what their habits are.

Competition

The **competition** you will face is very important unless you offer something unique (a **unique selling point**). You have to be honest with yourself here. Unique isn't just unique because you say so. It has to be a truly different and memorable product or experience.

Going back to the café scenario, if there are ten cafes within a 20-block radius, a café might not be your best option for a business unless you can offer an experience that customers want and can't get anywhere else. This is why carrying out a **Competitor Analysis** is so important.

Competitor Analysis

It isn't just about how many businesses like yours are in your market area. It is also about researching their products and services. Maybe there are a bunch of cafes, but none offer free-trade coffee. If you're analyzing a neighborhood where something like that is important to the **target market**, you have a **niche** you can fill. This is where research comes in and why it is important to be thorough.

Revenue

Revenue is the money that flows into a company from selling products, merchandise, and services. **Revenue**

also includes earnings from interest or rent received for property ownership.

If we are talking about the **revenues** generated by different companies or areas within one company, it can be used in the plural form (**revenues**).

Assets

Assets are a company's most valuable resource. They represent the fruits of past transactions and events and anything legally claimed by the business, such as money or property rights in another person's name (like **intellectual properties**). An **asset** is something with **economic value** to its owner; it has future benefits too!

Net Profit

Net Profit is the **revenue** generated after taking off all **costs**. **Net Income** or **Net Profit** helps determine overall **profitability**, reflecting how effectively the business has managed its **assets** to generate profit.

Gross Profit

Gross Profit measures a company's **profitability** without accounting for **overhead expenses** (electricity, gas, water, and other recurring bills).

It can be calculated by subtracting the **Cost of Goods Sold** (how much you directly paid for your products) from **Revenue** for that same period, making it a critical indicator of future success!

Break-Even Point

The **break-even point** is where **total revenues** are equal to **total costs**. It's an essential concept because it can help you figure out whether or not your business will be **profitable**, at least in the short term.

Cash flow

Cash flow is the money that enters and leaves a business. The **Net Cash Flow** for a period can be found by taking the **Initial Cash Balance** (money you have in the bank at the start of the period) and subtracting the **Closing Balance** (money you have in the bank at the end of the period).

Fixed Costs

Fixed costs, like rent and salaries, won't change if the company sells more. The opposite of **Fixed Costs** is **Variable Costs**. **Variable Costs** can change according to how many times they're used or produced; for example, wages may increase with increased **production rates** due to the payment of overtime or due to the employment of extra temporary staff to meet the increase in demand. This variable cost would decrease when there was less work needed.

Profit Margin

A company's **profit margin** is the percentage of each sale that results in **net income**. A high number means the business is having an easier time making money. In contrast, a low number suggests it might be difficult for them to turn enough **revenue** into **profits**, perhaps due to **competition** from other companies offering similar products or services with lower prices overall.

Overheads

Overheads are business costs that we cannot trace to a **specific cost per unit** produced or activity, but instead, we must pay on an ongoing basis regardless of whether we are selling products. Examples of this are insurance, rent, and utility bills.

STAKEHOLDERS

Anyone with a vested interest in a business. For instance, these can be shareholders, managers, directors, staff, or suppliers.

Chapter Review Exercise

Instructions: Read definitions 1-18 and fill the blank space with the business term from this chapter that best describes the meaning. You can check your answers on the next page after the exercise.

1. Anyone with a vested interest in a business is referred to as a ………………………. For instance, these can be shareholders, managers, directors, staff, or suppliers.

2. ………………… products and services is vital before launching them. Whether it is a service or product, you need to do this before launching. This is like creating a prototype before you start selling anything.

3. .... is a specific group of people who like a certain thing, or in other words, a specific section of the market.

4. All relevant data relating to your customers and their region is classed as .... This includes but is not limited to age, gender, level of education, income, interests, race, ethnicity/ cultural background, religion, marital status, etc.

5. Your .... is the specific section of the market that would be interested in your product or service.

6. The .... you will face is very important unless you offer something truly unique (a unique selling point).

7. .... describes the experience that a company provides. How does the company improve its customers' lives? What does it bring to the market?

8. .... is the revenue generated after taking off all costs.

9. .... is the money that flows into a company from the sale of products, merchandise, and services.

10. An .... is something with economic value to its owner

11. .... is also about researching your competitors' products and services.

12. The .... is where total revenues are equal to total costs. It's an essential concept because it can help you figure out whether or not your business will be profitable, at least in the short term.

13. .... is the measure of a company's profitability without accounting for overhead expenses (electricity, gas, water, and other recurring bills). It can be calculated by subtracting the Cost of Goods Sold (how much you directly paid for your products) from Revenue for that same period, making it a critical indicator of future success!

14. .... is the money that enters and leaves a business.

15. The .... for a period can be found by taking the Initial Cash Balance (money you have in the bank at the start of the period) and subtracting the Closing Balance (money you have in the bank at the end of the period).

16. A company's .... is the percentage of each sale that results in net income. A high number means the business is having an easier time making money.

17. ...., like rent and salaries, won't change if the company sells more. The opposite of this is Variable Costs. Variable Costs can change according to how many times they're used or produced; for example, wages may increase with increased production rates due to the payment of overtime or due to the employment of extra temporary staff to meet the increase in demand. This variable cost would decrease when there was less work needed.

18. ……………………………………… are business costs that we cannot trace to a specific cost per unit produced or activity, but instead, we must pay on an ongoing basis regardless of whether we are selling products or not. Examples of this are insurance, rent, and utility bills.

Answers

1. Anyone with a vested interest in a business is referred to as a **stakeholder**. For instance, these can be shareholders, managers, directors, staff, or suppliers.
2. **'Testing'** products and services is vital before launching them. Whether it is a service or product, you need to do this before launching. This is like creating a prototype before you start selling anything.
3. **A niche** is a specific group of people who like a certain thing, or in other words, a specific section of the market.
4. All relevant data relating to your customers and their region is classed as **demographics**. This includes but is not limited to age, gender, level of education, income, interests, race, ethnicity/cultural background, religion, marital status, etc.

5. Your **target customer** is the specific market section that would be interested in your product or service.
6. The **competition** you will face is very important unless you offer something unique (a unique selling point).
7. **Value' in business** describes the experience that a company provides. How does the company improve its customers' lives? What does it bring to the market?
8. **Net Profit** is the revenue generated after taking off all costs.
9. **Revenue** is the money that flows into a company from selling products, merchandise, and services.
10. An **asset** is something with economic value to its owner
11. **Competitor analysis** is also about researching your competitors' products and services.
12. The **break-even point** is where total revenues are equal to total costs. It's an essential concept because it can help you figure out whether or not

your business will be profitable, at least in the short term.

13. **Gross Profit** measures a company's profitability without accounting for overhead expenses (electricity, gas, water, and other recurring bills). It can be calculated by subtracting the Cost of Goods Sold (how much you directly paid for your products) from Revenue for that same period, making it a critical indicator of future success!

14. **Cash flow** is the money that enters and leaves a business.

15. The **Net Cash Flow** for a period can be found by taking the Initial Cash Balance (money you have in the bank at the start of the period) and subtracting the Closing Balance (money you have in the bank at the end of the period).

16. A company's **profit margin** is the percentage of each sale that results in net income. A high number means the business is having an easier time making money.

17. **Fixed costs**, like rent and salaries, won't change if the company sells more. The opposite of this is

Variable Costs. Variable Costs can change according to how many times they're used or produced; for example, wages may increase with increased production rates due to the payment of overtime or due to the employment of extra temporary staff to meet the increase in demand. This variable cost would decrease when there was less work needed.

18. **Overheads** are business costs that we cannot trace to a specific cost per unit produced or activity, but instead, we must pay on an ongoing basis regardless of whether we are selling products. Examples of this are insurance, rent, and utility bills.

CHAPTER 2. PRODUCTION CYCLES & PROCESSES

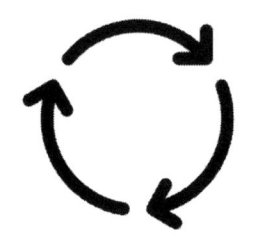

DESCRIBING SEQUENCES

The following linking words and phrases in the box **can** describe a sequence.

before / prior to	At first / firstly/ initially
following that/ after that / next / then/ when	as soon as/ once / immediately after/ in turn
before	after
where	At the same time- simultaneously
finally	

VOCABULARY EXERCISES

Exercise One

Highlight or underline the linking words in A-G and decide which is the first step in the sequence. Once you have done this, decide what is described and put the sentences in order.

- A. If it's being refurbished, the faulty components of the device are repaired in the factory
- B. and the tablet is then returned to the shop as a refurbished product.
- C. Once the device breaks, it is either discarded or refurbished.
- D. They are then assembled at a different factory
- E. First, the computer processors for the tablets are manufactured in an outsourced factory.
- F. Then they are sent to the central warehouse for distribution around the country

G. Simultaneously, the exterior and the memory chip are produced.

Exercise Two

Match 1 to 6 below with a sentence or phrase A-F to complete sequence descriptions. Please note that each full sentence belongs to a different process description.

1. As soon as the bricks have been formed
2. After fermentation,
3. Once the oranges are ripe, they are collected,
4. The water then flows into the penstock, which is a narrow chamber,
5. When the plant reaches a certain width, the leaves are picked.
6. In the early stages of milk production, cows graze in the field and are subsequently (then afterward) taken to a milking machine twice a day.

A. the chocolate is placed into molds and left to cool down.
B. The raw product is then heated to a high temperature to kill bacteria and make it safe for human consumption. Following this, it is put into refrigeration storage.
C. and they are then spread (laid) out on a large (industrial-sized) tray to enable them to dry under the sun.
D. they are left to dry.
E. they are then dried, sorted, blended, and packaged, ready for distribution to retailers.
F. and increases the pressure until the turbine turns.

Answers

Exercise 1

Linking words: if, and, then, once, then, first, simultaneously.

The lifecycle of a tablet computer is described.

E, G, D, F, C, A, B

Exercise 2

1d, 2a, 3c, 4f, 5e, 6b

Some Essential Vocabulary for Processes

Noun	Verb
Storage	Store
Pasteurization	Pasteurize
Harvest – harvesting	Harvest
Delivery	Deliver
Assembly	Assemble
Packing -Packaging	Pack - Package

Exercise Three

Read the process described on the next page and fill in the blanks with the missing word or phrase.

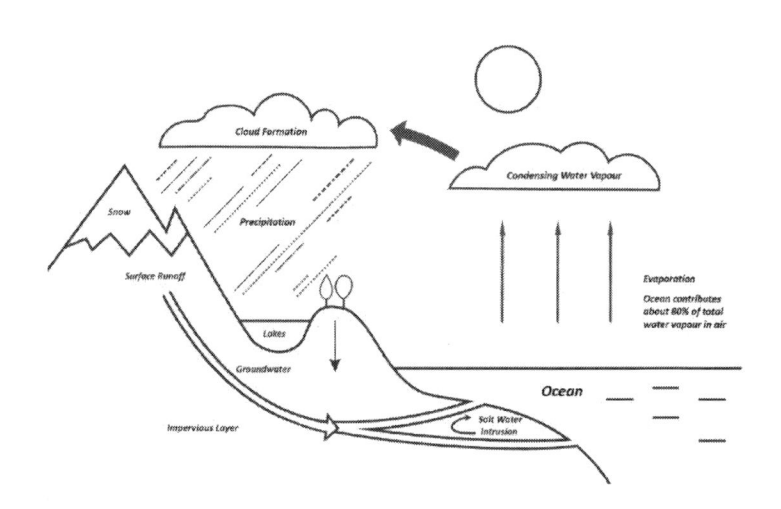

Diagram adapted from Nasa
https://gpm.nasa.gov/education/water-cycle

The diagram .... the water cycle. Firstly, water .... from the sea and floats into the atmosphere, ... **(two words)** accumulates in clouds and cools and condenses into rain or snow. The next stage shows the water's journey after falling to the ground, ... ends with .... **(three words)**

In the first stage of the ...., water, approximately 80% of which comes from Oceans, ... into the air as a result of the heat of the sun. After ...., the water vapor condenses to form clouds. An .... 80% of the water vapor comes from Oceans.

In the next ...., as clouds accumulate condensation, they produce precipitation in the form of rain and snow. A large part of the water from the precipitation falls into lakes or is .... by the ground.

The groundwater then .... back to the ocean without reaching the impervious layer through surface runoff.

................, Ocean water seeps through to the freshwater aquifers during the process is saltwater intrusion.

Answers

The diagram **illustrates** the water cycle. Firstly, water **evaporates** from the sea and floats into the atmosphere, **where it** accumulates in clouds and cools and condenses into rain or snow. The next stage shows the water's journey after falling to the ground, **which** ends with **saltwater intrusion**.

In the first stage of the **process**, water, approximately 80% of which comes from Oceans, **evaporates** into the air as a result of the heat of the sun. After **this**, the water vapor condenses to form clouds. An **estimated** 80% of the water vapor comes from Oceans.

In the next **stage**, as clouds accumulate condensation, they produce precipitation in the form of rain and snow. A large part of the water from the precipitation falls into lakes or is **absorbed** by the ground.

The groundwater **flows** back to the ocean without reaching the impervious layer through surface runoff.

Finally, Ocean water seeps through to the freshwater aquifers during saltwater intrusion.

CHAPTER 3. LINE GRAPH VOCABULARY

Let's focus on expanding your range of vocabulary and grammar structures for summarising changes that can take place within a line graph.

Vocabulary Exercises

Exercise 1

Match the words with their corresponding images below. More than one option is possible.

A. Rose steadily/increased steadily/grew steadily

B. Rose dramatically/increased dramatically/grew dramatically

C. Plummeted to/Plunged to ...

D. Hit a peak of, peaked at, or reached a high of ...

E. Fluctuated, varied, or oscillated/Became erratic. Was erratic/inconsistent

F. Dropped/Shrank/Fell drastically/ sharply dramatically

G. Remained flat/unchanged/stable / constant at

H. Dropped and then stabilized/evened out at

I. Hit a low of .../ bottomed out at

J. Dropped and then quickly recovered

K. Dipped/ Declined slightly before quickly recovering

L. Rocketed / Soared

M. Fell slowly/ gradually / steadily

1 ....

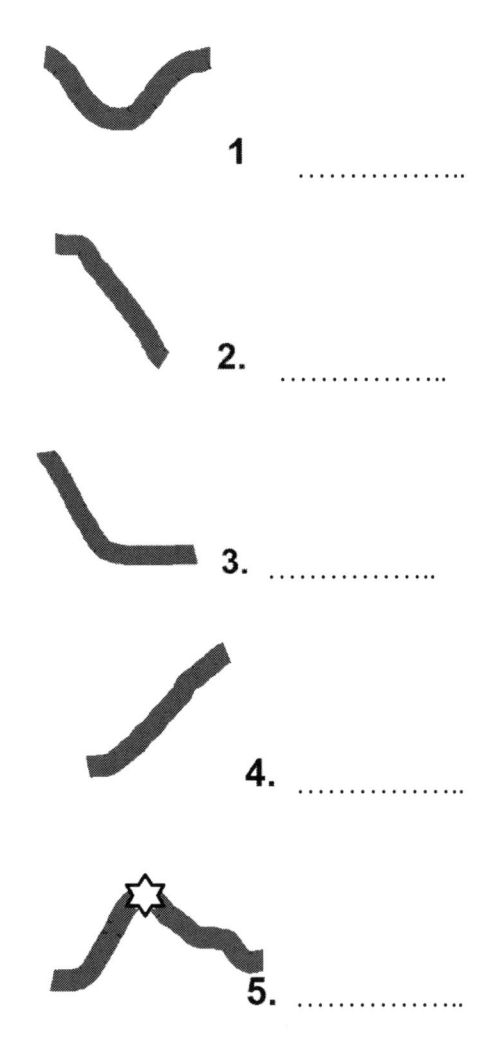

2. ....

3. ....

4. ....

5. ....

6. ....

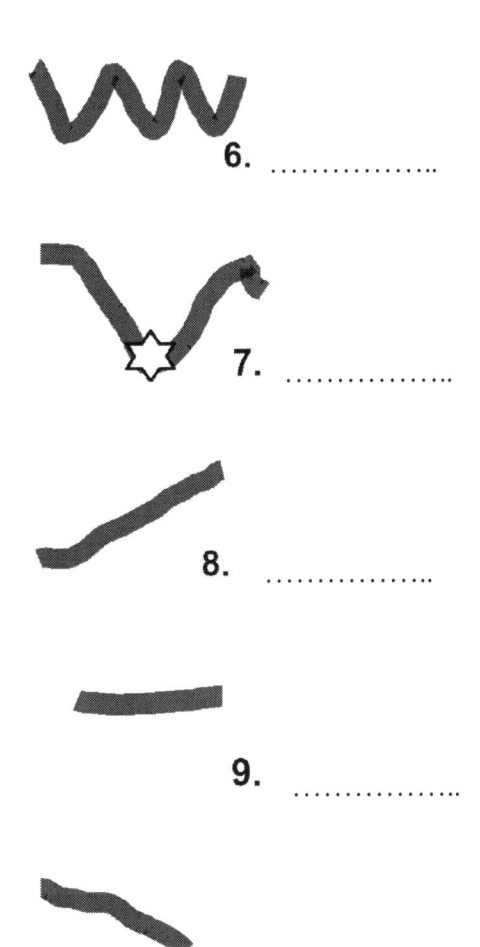

7. ....

8. ....

9. ....

10. ....

Answers

1 *Fell and then quickly recovered / Dipped/ fell slightly*

2 *Fell/dropped/shrank drastically/ dramatically / sharply/ Plummeted to/Plunged to*

3 *Dropped and then leveled off/evened out at*

4 *Rose/increased dramatically/Soared/ Rocketed*

5 *Hit a peak / Peaked at/reached a high of*

6 *Fluctuated/ was erratic*

7 *Hit a low of ...*

8 *Rose/increased steadily/ Rose/increased gradually*

9 *Remained flat/constant/unchanged/stable at*

10 *Fell gradually / steadily*

Please note that these are only some of the options from the table.

Definitions for some of the words

Word	Explanation
Dipped	Fell slightly but recovered quickly
Bottomed out / Hit a low of	The lowest point on the graph
Plummeted to…/ Plunged to	Suffered a quick and drastic or shocking decrease. Fell extremely quickly. A drastic fall or reduction
Fluctuated/ was erratic	Increases and decreases randomly, irregularly, or unpredictably
Rose/increased dramatically/ Soared/ Rocketed	Increased very quickly and drastically
Peaked at /	The highest point on the graph

reached a high of	
Remained constant/unchanged/stable at ..../ Leveled off/evened out at ...	a part of the graph where there is no change

Business Graph Exercise 2

The graph below gives information about changes in the birth and death rates in New Zealand between 1901 and 2101.

Summarise the information by selecting and reporting the main features, and make comparisons where relevant.

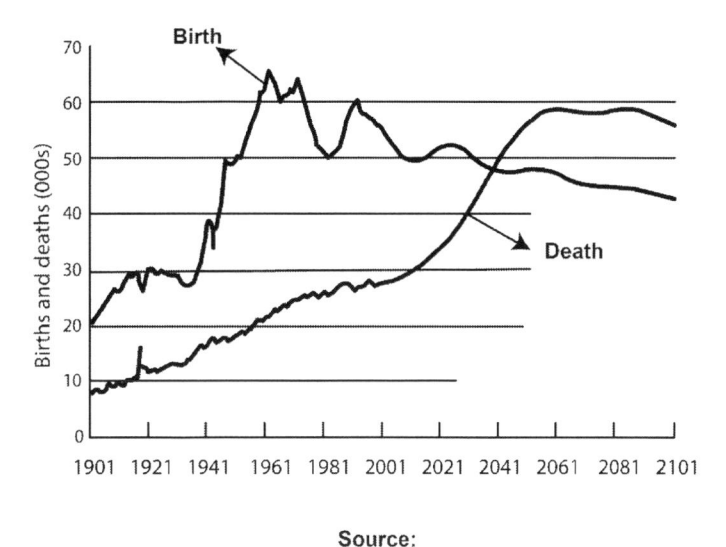

Source:

http://archive.stats.govt.nz/browse_for_stats/population/estimates_and_projections/changing-face-of-nzs-population.aspx

Fill in the blanks with appropriate language to describe the changes observed in the graph above:

The line graph shows the historical and predicted trends for the rate of birth and mortality in New Zealand for the period from 1901 through to 2101.

At the start of the review period, the birth rate surpasses the mortality rate. The forecasted data shows that the mortality rate is likely to exceed the birth rate by 2041, at which point, the large gap between the two will ....

At the beginning of the period, the birth rate started at 20,000, ... at around 66,000 in 1961, before .... between 50,000 and 65,000 until 2021. It is anticipated to .... to around 45,000 births by 2101 slowly.

In contrast, the mortality rate started at just below 10,000 in 1901 and .... (two words), reaching around 30,000 in 2021. This .... is expected to accelerate between 2021 and 2041, when the number of deaths will surpass the number of births. By 2051 the

60

death rate will .... at around 60,000 and .... marginally until the end of the period.

Answers

The line graph shows the historical and predicted trends for the rate of birth and mortality in New Zealand for the period from 1901 through to 2101.

At the start of the review period, the birth rate surpasses the mortality rate. The forecasted data shows that the mortality rate is likely to exceed the birth rate by 2041, at which point, the large gap between the two will level off.

At the beginning of the period, the birth rate started at 20,000, peaking at around 66,000 in 1961, before fluctuating between 50,000 and 65,000 until 2021. It is anticipated to decline to around 45,000 births by 2101 slowly.

In contrast, the mortality rate started at just below 10,000 in 1901 and steadily rose, reaching around 30,000 in 2021. This increase is expected to accelerate between 2021 and 2041, when deaths will surpass the number of births. By 2051 the death rate will stabilize at around 60,000 and decline marginally until the end of the period.

EXPRESSIONS FOR LINE GRAPHS

- *...significantly declined...*
- *...remained the same...*
- *...reached a plateau...*
- *...rose dramatically...*
- *...fell slightly...*
- *...fluctuated...*
- *...increased steadily...*
- *...fell gradually...*
- *...decreased steadily...*
- *...remained stable...*
- *...recovered...*
- *...fluctuated dramatically...*
- *...rocketed...*
- *...plunged...*
- *...a dramatic fall...*
- *...a period of stability...*

- *...a slight dip...*
- *...it doubled...*
- *...it halved...*
- *...increased sevenfold (7 times)*
- *...increased fourfold (4 times)*
- *...proved to be the most popular...*
- *...began the year higher; however, by the end of the year ...*
- *...followed the same sales trend...*
- *...were consistently the lowest...*
- *...A similar pattern is also noted on...*
- *...With regards to...*
- *...is similar/ dissimilar...*

STRUCTURES FOR SUMMARISING CHANGE

If you want to achieve great results, you need to learn more than just one structure for summarizing change. You must add an element of variety to your communication when describing shifts in data. This will keep your reader or listener engaged, but it will also help you communicate more efficiently, and it will give a better impression of your abilities as a professional.

Be mindful of using the correct word forms when building your sentences. Lapses in concentration can cause some writers to confuse adjectives such as *"progressive"* with their adverb form *"progressively."*

The following resource tables contain the language to describe any graph that involves changes over time.

There + be + adjective + noun + in + noun
There was a slow rise in the number of kilograms consumed.
There was a dramatic rise in the amount of oil produced.
There was a sharp jump in ice cream sales
There has been a considerable increase in the number of languages spoken within the region since 1980.
There was a slight increase in the number of cars sold.
There was a sharp fall in the number of loans offered.
There was a dramatic fluctuation in the amount of rice consumed.

Noun + verb + adverb
Fast food consumption rose steadily.
The number of people claiming unemployment benefits rose considerably between 2008 and 2011.
The value of gold decreased slightly during the period.
The figures declined slightly, dropping to 44,000 in 2012.

Time + saw/experienced/witnessed + adjective + noun + in + noun
*there is no preposition before time words in this structure (Never: *In* + time + *saw*…)
2003 saw a gradual increase in oil consumption.
2009 saw a sudden plunge in ice-cream sales to 20,000.
The end of the period saw a gradual decline in the figures, dropping to 44,000 in 2012.
The decade ended pretty much the same as it began, with an average consumption of just over 20lb per household.

Adding Transitions to Your Sentences

The U.S. produces over 2.2 billion tons of wheat every year. **In contrast***, Russia produces just over half a billion per year.*

Italy produced large amounts of dairy products. **In comparison***, Thailand produced very little.*

Finland imports some 10 million tons of flour per year **but** *produces none.*

Note: remember the word *some* can be used to mean *about/ around,* so you can use it to add some variety to your writing.

WHILE/WHEREAS/ALTHOUGH/THOUGH

These words are great for adding transitions within sentences without adding a full stop and writing a new sentence. They allow you to compare and contrast while keeping your text fluid and readable.

Although *Italy produces over 6 million tons of olives, Spain produces almost double that amount.*

Spain produces high levels of solar power, ***whereas/while*** *Japan produces almost none.*

While *Germany consumes nearly 80 million tons of rice per year, it produces none.*

COMPARING AND CONTRASTING SIMILAR DATA

Austria produced **the same** amount of butter as Switzerland.

Like Thailand, Malaysia produces 30,000 bottles.

India consumes over 100 million tons of rice per year; **Likewise,/ Similarly**, China consumes 118.8 million.

Both India and China consume over 100 million tons of rice per year.

Both the U.K. and Spain produce medium levels of carbon emissions.

CHAPTER 4. BAR CHART VOCABULARY

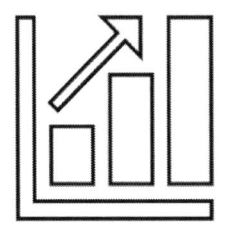

Exercise

Read the text on the next page and notice the gaps.

Put the terms in **bold** in the right gap within the text. Then, check your answers on the next page.

remained relatively stable

To begin,

levels

will see little change

Whereas

while

However

Around

remaining slightly higher overall

accounted for

…………….., in 2010, the Online Retail industry started at 11%, ……….. the Highstreet Retail industry ……………… 7% of total investment.

During the next decade, the ………….. for both industries …………………………… at ……………15% and 8%, with the Online Retail sector ……………………………………, despite a small decrease between 2019 and 2020.

……………………, a considerable change is expected between the two categories in the next ten years. Investment in the Online Retail sector will increase dramatically to 33% by 2025 and then nearly 45% in 2030, ……………… the Highstreet Retail sector ……………………….., increasing to only 10%.

Answers

*In 2010, the Online Retail industry started at 11%, **whereas** the Highstreet Retail industry **accounted for** 7% of total investment.*

*During the next decade, the **levels** for both industries **remained relatively stable** at **around** 15% and 8%, with the Online Retail sector **remaining slightly higher overall**, despite a small decrease between 2019 and 2020.*

***However**, a considerable change is expected between the two categories in the next ten years. Investment in the Online Retail sector will increase dramatically to 33% by 2025 and then nearly 45% in 2030, **while** the Highstreet Retail sector **will see little change**, increasing to only 10%.*

CHAPTER 5. NUMBERS, PERCENTAGES & FRACTIONS

Expressing Approximations

Re-phrase sentences a-i using the vocabulary in the list below. You can make any necessary changes. There are four expressions you won't need to use.

The bulk of

the lowest percentages

was noticeably higher

a smaller proportion of

was significantly higher

had the lowest percentages

had slightly higher figures

a third of the number of

40% of

Over 75%

Three times the number of

the largest proportion of

One in four

a) The Oasis concert was attended by three times as many people as the Blur concert.
b) More than four out of ten people chose to use trains.
c) The largest proportion of purchases came from Germany as opposed to Spain.
d) A quarter of customers ordered print rather than digital products.
e) The website lost just under three-quarters of its visitors compared to last year.
f) Consumers in all countries spent more on toys than any other product category.
g) Consumers spent the least on leisure in all countries.
h) Consumers in Turkey and Ireland spent much more on food, drinks, and tobacco than consumers in the other countries.
i) Spending on clothing and footwear was a lot higher in Portugal, at 10%, than in the rest of the countries.

Write below

a) ....
   ....
b) ....
   ....
c) ....
   ....
d) ....
   ....
e) ....
   ....
f) ....
   ....
g) ....
   ....
h) ....
   ....
i) ....
   ....

Suggested Answers

a) The Oasis concert was attended by **three times the number of** many people as the Blur concert.

b) More than **40% of** people chose to use trains.

c) **The bulk of** purchases came from Germany as opposed to Spain.

d) **One in four** customers ordered print rather than digital products.

e) The social media website lost just **under 75%** of its visitors compared to last year.

f) **The largest proportion** of spending in all countries was on toys.

g) The leisure/education category has **the lowest percentages** in the table.

h) Consumer spending on food, drinks, and tobacco **was noticeably higher** in Turkey and Ireland than in the other countries.

i) Spending on clothing and footwear **was significantly higher** in Portugal, at 10%, than in other countries.

PERCENTAGES & FRACTIONS

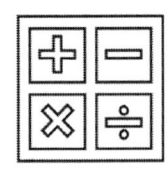

When describing percentages and fractions, it can often be good to alternate between the two, so you can keep things interesting and varied. You should also use phrases to show when a number is not exact, such as *'roughly,' 'just under,'* or *'just over,'* for example.

Here are some language examples to increase your flexibility when describing pie charts:

80% / four-fifths

75% / three-quarters

70% / seven in ten

5% 65% /   two-thirds

60% / three-fifths

55% / more than half

50% / half

45% / more than two fifths

40% / two-fifths

35% / more than a third

30% / less than a third

25% / a quarter

20% / one fifth (a fifth)

15% / less than a/one fifth

10% / one in ten

5% /   one in twenty

Percentage Qualifier

77%   just over three quarters

77%   approximately three quarters

49%   just under a half

49%   nearly a half

32%   almost a third

Percentage proportion / number / amount / majority / minority

75% - 85%   a very large majority

65% - 75%   a significant proportion

10% - 15%   a minority

5%   a very small number

CHAPTER 6. PUBLIC SPEAKING & TRAINING

LANGUAGE FOR TEACHING & PRESENTING

How to Introduce Your Session

1. *Good morning/afternoon/evening ....*
2. *It's an absolute pleasure to welcome all of you here today for (insert purpose of meeting or presentation)*
3. *I'm ... (insert name + job title needed)*
4. *By the time we finish this presentation/ meeting/ training session, you will be able to (insert learning objectives here)*

Introduce the session/presentation topic

I will be focusing on (insert focus of session here)

Outline

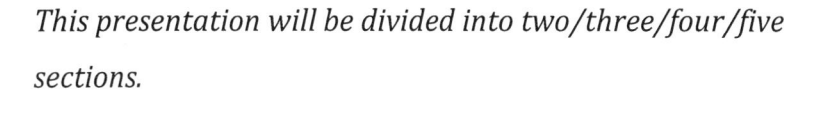

This presentation will be divided into two/three/four/five sections.

Firstly, ...

Secondly,....

Thirdly, ...

The fourth section will look at ......

Lastly, /Finally, / The last section will look at ....

Your Questions Policy

Please feel free to put your hand up if you have any questions.

OR

After we finish, there will be ten minutes for you to ask me any questions you have. OPTIONAL: If you come up with any questions after the session is over, please feel free to email me with them. My email address is at the bottom of the training manual.

Main Body

Once you've finished the introductory section of your presentation, you should aim to smoothly go into the main part of the talk.

Beginning

Now let's turn to the first section of this presentation, where we will focus on (insert what you will concentrate on here)

So, firstly...

To start with...

To begin with......

Concluding a Section Inside the Main Body

That finishes the section on (insert topic of section)...

Okay, we've looked at (insert topic of section)...

Starting a New Section

Let's look at the next section/area/part/module/unit, which is...

Listing & Sequencing

Listing

Factors

There are ... two/three/four/several... factors to consider/bear in mind.... Firstly... Secondly... Thirdly... Finally,.../Lastly,...

Types or Categories

There are two/three/four types of ......

Communicating Pros & Cons

There are pros and cons to this approach.

The pros are (insert advantages here using "firstly, secondly, etc."))....

The cons are (insert disadvantages here using "firstly, secondly, etc.")....

Sequences

Steps

There are four steps we must take. The first step is... The second step is...

Phases/Stages

There are two/three/four/five etc., different phases to the process.

Ending the Session

Closing the Presentation

Okay, this ends the final part of the presentation/training session.

To wrap things up,...

Conclusion

I'd like to finish by emphasizing the importance of X, Y, and Z.....

To conclude, ...

In conclusion, ...

I recommend/suggest that we...

Questions and/or Discussion Time

We now have (insert amount of time) for any questions and discussion.

Now I'd be interested to hear your thoughts/suggestions/ideas/questions etc.

Thanking Your Audience

I'd like to thank all of you for taking the time to be here today.

Thank you for coming today. It's been a real pleasure.

MEETINGS & DISCUSSIONS

Putting your reasons in order	Firstly/Secondly. Thirdly/Finally
Expressing an opinion	I hold the view that ... In my view... It is probably true to say that.... There can be no doubt that ...
Mentioning what other people think	It has been suggested that.... There are those who believe that... There are those who argue that... Opponents/ supporters of

	(e.g., hunting) ... argue that.... Most people hold firmly to the belief that... It is often claimed that...
Common opinions in society	It is widely believed/thought that Few people would contest that.... Nobody would dispute the fact that .... It is generally agreed that...
Referring to evidence and facts	Research suggests that... All the evidence suggests that ... Recent evidence indicates that .....
Changing direction	However/Nevertheless

Giving examples	For example
	for instance
	such as
Concluding	In conclusion / Overall,

Exercise One

Read the beginning of the presentation. Fill the gaps with an appropriate word or phrase from the box (You don't need to use all of them):

To conclude	I hold the view that	however.	Firstly, research/our data suggests that
may	which can lead to	For instance,	when people
they are more likely to	Secondly, few people would contest that	Therefore	it is likely that
Finally,	such as	However, there are those who argue that	nobody would contest the fact that
In addition, it is often claimed that	Nobody would dispute the fact that	there can be no doubt that	Hence,

1. ....
   many government initiatives create inefficiencies
   .... gaps
   in the market.

2. .... we
   should be investing more in trying to exploit
   these gaps in the market, ...
   many people disagree with this opinion. In the
   next 30 to 40 minutes, we will examine the
   issues, and I will try to convince you that we are
   currently missing out on some of the biggest
   opportunities available in the sector. *(Note: to
   miss out on means when you don't take
   advantage of an opportunity)

3. ....,(a)
   ....(b) over
   70% of government initiatives create new
   inefficiencies, and that the companies in the
   sectors which could solve these new problems
   take an average of 12 months to react.

4. ………………………… last year's biggest projects all came from problems caused by government initiatives; we lost three contracts that we could have won if we had approached the clients sooner. If we can provide agencies with early, reliable information and solutions ……………………………………………………………… react positively and award us the contracts.

Answers

1. **Nobody would dispute the fact that** many government initiatives create inefficiencies **that can lead to** gaps in the market.

2. **I hold the view that (a)** we should be investing more in trying to exploit these gaps in the market; **however, (b)** many people disagree with this opinion. In the next 30 to 40 minutes, we will examine the issues, and I will try to convince you that we are currently missing out on some of the biggest opportunities available in the sector.
    *(Note: to **miss out on** means when you don't take advantage of an opportunity)

3. **Firstly**, **research suggests that** over 70% of government initiatives create new inefficiencies and that the companies in the sectors which could solve these new problems take an average of 12 months to react.

4. **For instance**, last year's biggest projects all came from problems caused by government initiatives; we lost three contracts that we could have won if

we had approached the clients sooner. If we can provide agencies with early, reliable information and solutions, **they are more likely to** react positively and award us the contracts.

CHAPTER 7. COMMONLY CONFUSED WORDS

Affect – influence (verb)

Effect – a change (noun)

Poor time management can affect your work performance.

Poor time management can have a significant effect on your work performance.

Whether – this is used to show an alternative in an indirect question

Weather – the condition of the atmosphere in an area

I'm not sure whether the project should go ahead.

I'm sure that the meeting is going to go smoothly tomorrow.

Uninterested – when someone is bored by something or doesn't have any motivation to pay attention to it.

Disinterested - neutral

She is obviously uninterested in this job; she makes minimal effort to learn anything new.

I think journalists should be impartial representatives of public opinion.

Loose – not fixed or contained.

Lose – to experience defeat or to misplace something

These trousers are too loose; I need a size smaller.

We cannot lose that client. We have to fix the problem quickly!

Cite - to quote a source of information

Sight – the ability to see. Also, "a sight" is something that can be seen.

Site – a place

It's important to cite a variety of sources in your marketing reports.

He lost sight in one eye in his old age.

This would be an excellent site for the new factory.

Allowed – permitted

Aloud – to speak in a voice loud enough for others to hear

We are not allowed to leave the house during the quarantine.

He was visibly nervous as he read the words aloud.

Comprise - consist of or be composed of.

Compose - to constitute

The new office comprises ten meeting rooms and two bathrooms.

The new office is composed of ten meeting rooms and two bathrooms.

Accept - agree to receive or do something

Except - preposition meaning 'not including.'

I would like you to accept the job.

All her colleagues attended the meeting except Kelly.

Elicit – to bring out or provoke a reaction.

Illicit – illegal or frowned upon

The presenter elicited answers from the audience before explaining the solution.

The director was suspended pending an investigation into his alleged participation in illicit activities.

Imply - To express something without saying it directly

Infer – to come to a conclusion based on the evidence available

He was implying that she could not handle the job.

From what she said, we were able to infer that she had the situation under control.

Incredible – impressive, astonishing

Incredulous – unsure, or not believing something

The size of the new project is incredible.

He was incredulous when he first heard about the size of the new project.

Historic -a standout event in history.

Historical – related to history.

Columbus set sail with his team of Spanish explorers in his historic voyage, searching for China and India.

I donated some historical reference books to the local library last week.

Assert - to affirm.

Ensure - to make sure

Assure - to try to reduce someone's fear or worry by saying something positive

She asserted that there was financial espionage going on.

We wanted to ensure that the project would be finished before the deadline.

She assured us that the project would be completed on time.

Complement – to add to or complete something

Compliment – to give praise

The sauce complements the meat perfectly.

The financial director complimented John on his handling of the crisis.

CHAPTER 8. COMMON CORPORATE TERMS

KPI (KEY PERFORMANCE INDICATOR): the core metrics used to measure a person, department, or company's overall performance.

EXAMPLES OF KPIs:

CUSTOMER ACQUISITION COST (how much does the company pay to acquire each new customer? This can include marketing costs, overheads, etc.)

CUSTOMER LIFETIME VALUE: how much is each customer worth to the company on average over their lifetime?

CUSTOMER SATISFACTION SCORE: how do customers rate your company? (this is usually measured using data from surveys or similar)

SALES TARGET % (FORECAST/ACTUAL) ...

Forecast: What change in sales does the company predict this month/quarter/year?

Actual: what was the real-world result at the end of the period?

REVENUE PER CUSTOMER: what is the average revenue received from each customer?

ROA (RETURN ON ASSETS): what revenue does the business receive from its assets?

CURRENT RATIO (ASSETS/LIABILITIES): what is the ratio of assets to liabilities? (things you own VS things you owe)

EMPLOYEE EXPERIENCE refers to an employee's overall experience at the company. It includes every interaction with the company, from training to appraisals.

EMPLOYEE ENGAGEMENT refers to the level of connection between an employee and a company. It describes the level of affinity, enthusiasm, and motivation that the employee feels.

EMPLOYEE SATISFACTION: How happy and motivated are employees?

PSYCHOLOGICAL SAFETY:

- *Is risk-taking something viable at the company?*
- *Is it possible to learn from failure, or is it too risky?*

Businesses with strong levels of psychological safety encourage creative thinking and new initiatives. They tend to be more innovative.

CONSOLIDATION EXERCISE

Instructions:
Answer the following questions to review the vocabulary from this chapter.

1. What are KPIs?

2. ………………………………… = how much does the company pay to acquire each new customer? This can include marketing costs, overheads, etc.

3. .... measures how much each customer is worth to the company on average over their lifetime.

4. .... = how do customers rate your company? (this is usually measured using data from surveys or similar)

5. Sales Target % (Forecast/Actual)
   ....: What change in sales does the company predict this month/quarter/year?
   ....: what was the real-world result at the end of the period?

6. ....= what is the average revenue received from each customer?

7. ....= what revenue does the business receive as a result of its assets?

8. ....= what is the ratio of assets to liabilities? (things you own VS things you owe)

9. ....= this refers to an employee's overall experience at the company. It includes every interaction with the company, from training to appraisals.

10. ....= this refers to the level of connection between an employee and a company. It describes the level of affinity, enthusiasm, and motivation that the employee feels.

11. ....= How happy and motivated are employees?

12. Businesses with strong levels of .... encourage creative thinking and new initiatives. They tend to be more innovative.

Answers

1. **What are KPIs?** The core metrics used to measure a person, department, or company's overall performance.
2. **Customer Acquisition Cost** (how much does the company pay to acquire each new customer? This can include marketing costs, overheads, etc.)
3. **Customer Lifetime Value:** how much is each customer worth to the company on average over their lifetime?
4. **Customer Satisfaction Score:** how do customers rate your company? (this is usually measured using data from surveys or similar)
5. **Sales Target % (Forecast/Actual)**
    Forecast: What change in sales does the company predict this month/quarter/year?
    Actual: what was the real-world result at the end of the period?
6. **Revenue per Customer:** what is the average revenue received from each customer?
7. **ROA (Return on Assets):** what revenue does the business receive from its assets?

8. **Current Ratio (Assets/Liabilities):** what is the ratio of assets to liabilities? (things you own VS things you owe)
9. **Employee experience** refers to an employee's overall experience at the company. It includes every interaction with the company, from training to appraisals.
10. **Employee engagement** refers to the level of connection between an employee and a company. It describes the level of affinity, enthusiasm, and motivation that the employee feels.
11. **Employee satisfaction:** How happy and motivated are employees?
12. Businesses with strong levels of **psychological safety** encourage creative thinking and new initiatives. They tend to be more innovative.

OTHER CORPORATE TERMS:

TALENT MANAGEMENT: This work area focuses on getting the right people to take the organization towards its goals.

CHANGE MANAGEMENT: this focuses on administering the whole process of change. Change management involves effectively communicating with staff at all levels so that changes happen as smoothly as possible.

LEARNING & DEVELOPMENT (L&D): L&D focuses on providing the training needed to achieve the company's objectives.

GROWTH MINDSET: this describes a way of thinking in which people aim to constantly improve by continually striving to push boundaries, train, and learn from experience.

RETENTION: the measurement of how many employees stay at the company.

STAFF (EMPLOYEE) TURNOVER: how many employees leave the company on average during a specified period (monthly, yearly, etc.)

CORE VALUES: the central overarching values or moral compass of a company. What does the company stand for?

COMPANY MISSION: the purpose of the business. Why does it exist?

COMPANY VISION: Where does the company want to be in the future?

COMPANY CULTURE: the environment and atmosphere within a company. The personality of the company.

CULTURE FIT: similarity between the company's culture and the employees or project. Do the employees fit well into the environment within the company? Does the project fit in with the company's core values and culture?

DIVERSITY & INCLUSION (D&I): Diversity & Inclusion (D&I) programming aims to make the workplace accessible, safe, and equal for everyone, regardless of sex, gender, race, sexuality, or ability.

PERFORMANCE MANAGEMENT: this focuses on administering employee performance over time.

AD-HOC: on demand. When needed.

SYNC UP: a conversation between two or more people when needed. An impromptu meeting.

EMPLOYEE CHECK-IN: Quarterly performance conversations focusing on employee performance and objectives.

PERFORMANCE REVIEW involves periodically analyzing and evaluating employee performance and then setting improvement goals that align with the company's overall objectives.

360 FEEDBACK: this is an H.R. term referring to employee performance feedback taken from the employee, their managers, and colleagues. It uses as many relevant sources as possible.

OBJECTIVES AND KEY RESULTS (OKRS): business-wide objectives that can be measured and amended as needed.

EMPLOYEE APPRECIATION: The sense of value that staff receives from being recognized for good work.

CONSOLIDATION EXERCISE

Instructions:

Fill the blank spaces with the correct term to review the vocabulary from this chapter.

1. .... this area of work focuses on getting the right people to take the organization towards its goals.

2. .... involves effectively communicating with staff at all levels so that changes happen as smoothly as possible.

3. .... focuses on providing the training needed to achieve the company's objectives.

4. .... this describes a way of thinking in which people aim to constantly improve by continually striving to push boundaries, train, and learn from experience.

5. .... the measurement of how many employees stay at the company.

6. .... the measurement of how many employees leave the company on average during a specified period (monthly, yearly, etc.)

7. .... the central overarching values or moral compass of a company. What does the company stand for?

8. .... the purpose of the business. Why does it exist?

9. .... Where does the company want to be in the future?

10. .... the environment and atmosphere within a company. The personality of the company.

11. .... similarity between the company's culture and the employees or project. Do the employees fit well into the environment within the company? Does the project fit in with the company's core values and culture?

12. .... programming aims to make the workplace accessible, safe, and equal for everyone, regardless of sex, gender, race, sexuality, or ability.

13. .... this focuses on administering employee performance over time.

14. .... on demand. When needed.

15. ………………… a conversation between two or more people when needed. An impromptu meeting.

16. ……………………………… quarterly performance conversations focusing on employee performance and objectives.

17. ………………………………… this involves periodically analyzing and evaluating employee performance and then setting improvement goals that align with the company's overall objectives.

18. ……………………… this is an H.R. term referring to employee performance feedback taken from the employee, their managers, and colleagues. It uses as many relevant sources as possible.

19. ………………………………………… business-wide objectives that can be measured and amended as needed.

20. .... The sense of value that staff receives from being recognized for good work.

Answers

1. **Talent management:** This work area focuses on getting the right people to take the organization towards its goals.
2. **Change management** involves effectively communicating with staff at all levels so that changes happen as smoothly as possible.
3. **L&D** focuses on providing the training needed to achieve the company's objectives.
4. **Growth mindset:** this describes a way of thinking in which people aim to constantly improve by continually striving to push boundaries, train, and learn from experience.
5. **Retention:** the measurement of how many employees stay at the company.
6. **Staff (employee) turnover:** how many employees leave the company on average during a specified period (monthly, yearly, etc.)
7. **Core values:** the central overarching values or moral compass of a company. What does the company stand for?
8. **Company mission:** the purpose of the business. Why does it exist?

9. **Company vision:** Where does the company want to be in the future?
10. **Company culture:** the environment and atmosphere within a company. The personality of the company.
11. **Culture fit:** similarity between the company's culture and the employees or project. Do the employees fit well into the environment within the company? Does the project fit in with the company's core values and culture?
12. **Diversity & Inclusion (D&I)** programming aims to make the workplace accessible, safe, and equal for everyone, regardless of sex, gender, race, sexuality, or ability.
13. **Performance management:** this focuses on administering employee performance over time.
14. **Ad-hoc:** on demand. When needed.
15. **Sync up**: a conversation between two or more people when needed. An impromptu meeting.
16. **Employee check-in**: Quarterly performance conversations focusing on employee performance and objectives.
17. **Performance review** involves periodically analyzing and evaluating employee performance and then setting improvement goals that align with the company's overall objectives.

18. **360 feedback:** this is an H.R. term referring to employee performance feedback taken from the employee, their managers, and colleagues. It uses as many relevant sources as possible.
19. **Objectives and Key Results (OKRs):** business-wide objectives that can be measured and amended as needed.
20. **Employee appreciation:** The sense of value that staff receives from being recognized for good work.

CHAPTER 9.
PROFESSIONAL VERBS &
PHRASAL VERBS WITH
PRACTICE EXERCISES

A

Read the definitions for each phrasal verb in section A below and complete the exercise at the end of the section.

ABIDE BY means to accept or respect terms of an agreement, a law, a rule or a decision that has been made.

ACCEDE TO means to initially reject and then agree to a request after negotiation

ACCOUNT FOR means:

(1) to provide an explanation of how or why something happened.

(2) To be a specific or named portion of something.

(3) To keep a record of and monitor how resources are used in a business.

(4) To take into consideration when you are making a decision.

ACCOUNT TO: to pay to an individual or organisation together with a breakdown of the amount paid and how it is calculated.

ADHERE TO means to respect a particular law, rule, agreement or guidelines. (same as abide by)

AMOUNT TO means:

(1) to total or add up to.

(2) To be the same as.

APPERTAIN TO (OR PERTAIN TO) means to be related to or belong to something

EXERCISE 1

Now complete each sentence with the most appropriate word or words. You may need to change the form of the words to suit the sentence and you will need to use some words more than once.

"The figures………………… to last year's sales.".

"When X Ltd failed to deliver the goods as specified under the agreement, this ………………… to a breach of contract"

"Both parties have ………………… strictly to the terms of the contract".

"The defendant ………………… to the claimant for damages received."

"There are 265 Euros which have not been .... for, we need to review the numbers again".

"Food sales .... 22% of total revenue".

"The potential tax bill if the case was lost was .... when we made the decision".

"All parties must .... the terms of the agreement"

"Last year, the supplier eventually ....repeated requests for an increase in the line of credit".

"How can we ....the fact that the goods arrived late?"

"The debt .... to over €120,000".

B

Read the definitions for each term below and complete the exercise at the end of the section.

BREAK DOWN means:

(1) to separate information into several parts to make it easier to understand, analyse and discuss.

(2) To fail.

BREAK OFF means: (1) to stop negotiating or discussing

BREAK UP means: (1) the separation of a company or an organisation into smaller parts.

EXERCISE 2

Complete each sentence with the most appropriate word or words. You may need to change the form of the words to suit the sentence and you will need to use some words more than once.

"The agreement .... due to one party's excessive demands".

"We had to .... the meeting".

"The company was .... to make the sector more competitive"

"The numbers for the year .... as follows"

E

Read the definitions for each term below and complete the exercise at the end of the section.

ENTER INTO means (1) to begin or start a formal agreement; or (2) to start to deal with something.

ENTITLE TO (ADJ. ENTITLED TO) means to give the right to something.

EXCLUDE (noun form: an **exclusion**): When something is not covered, as in specific damage not covered in a contract.

EXERCISE 3

Complete each sentence with the most appropriate word or words. You may need to change the form of the words to suit the sentence and you will need to use some words more than once.

"Both parties shall have the right to seek to settle any dispute arising from the agreement by arbitration, which will .... any other form of dispute resolution."

"Ms. Temple .... negotiations with the factory to reach an agreement."

"Early termination of the contract ....the lender to compensation".

F

Read the definitions for each term below and complete the exercise.

FACTOR IN: to include or take into account when assessing, evaluating or planning something.

FIND IN FAVOUR OF/AGAINST (ALSO: RULE IN FAVOUR OF/AGAINST) is often used to describe the decision of the judge or jury in court.

EXERCISE 4

Complete each sentence with the most appropriate word or words. You may need to change the form of the words to suit the sentence and you will need to use some words more than once.

"The judge .... Mr. Right and awarded him compensation to the amount of £10,000"

"Using a computer programme they .... the costs of keeping the old machinery for the next three years"

H

Read the definitions for each term below and complete the exercise at the end of the section.

HAND DOWN:

(1) In inheritance, this phrasal verb means to give or leave something to someone else.

(2) When a judge or jury announce their official decision in a case.

Exercise 5

Complete each sentence with the most appropriate word or words. You may need to change the form of the words to suit the sentence and you will need to use some words more than once.

"The judge .... a suspended sentence"

"The land .... to him by his uncle, who died last year".

P

Read the definitions for each term below and complete the exercise at the end of the section.

PASS OFF means:

'Passing off' is also a type of tort, which for example restricts businesses from giving the impression that their goods or services are associated with another.

PROVIDE THAT...

If you are giving a detailed summary, paraphrasing, or repeating a particular law word for word, use "provide (s) that"

Exercise 6

Complete each sentence with the most appropriate word or words. You may need to change the form of the words to suit the sentence and you will need to use some words more than once.

"The law ………………….. that the penalty for a first offence can be up to 150 USD."

"She was accused of trying to ……………… her logo for another company's".

"The Regulations ……………………….. "traffic data" must be recorded and filed with the appropriate agency. "

S-Z

Read the definitions for each term below and complete the exercise at the end of the section.

SET FORTH is used before words such as rights, duties, obligations, and procedures:

STRIKE OUT means (1) this is when a judge suspends a case before the court date.

SUM UP. To sum up, means to summarise information. In legal English 'the summing up' in a trial with a jury, is when the judge summarises the evidence presented, in order to draw the attention of the jury to the most important points.

WEIGH UP is to evaluate evidence and arguments before making a decision.

EXERCISE 7

Complete each sentence with the most appropriate word or words. You may need to change the form of the words to suit the sentence and you will need to use some words more than once.

"The judge .... the evidence presented by both sides before the jury made their decision"

"The Regulation .... the procedure for processing and fulfilment of orders"

"Articles 12 and 22 can unite the parties and contribute to advancing regional priorities within the framework .... by the law."

"The judge can .... the case if she decides there finds no reasonable grounds"

"The following article .... the basic terms of the contract."

"The judge .... the evidence for over an hour before handing down her verdict."

ANSWERS

A

"The figures appertain to last year's sales.".

"When X Ltd failed to deliver the goods as specified under the agreement, this amounted to a breach of contract"

"Both parties have adhered strictly to the terms of the contract".

"The defendant accounted to the claimant for damages received."

"There are 265 Euros which have not been accounted for, we need to review the numbers again".

"Food sales accounted for 22% of total revenue".

"The potential tax bill if the case was lost was accounted for when we made the decision".

"All parties must abide by the terms of the agreement"

"Last year, the supplier eventually acceded to repeated requests for an increase in the line of credit".

"How can we account for the fact that the goods arrived late?"

"The debt amounted to over €120,000".

B

"The agreement broke down due to one party's excessive demands".

"We had to break off the meeting".

"The company was broken up to make the sector more competitive"

"The numbers for the year break down as follows"

E

"Both parties shall have the right to seek to settle any dispute arising from the agreement by arbitration, which will exclude any other form of dispute resolution."

"Ms. Temple entered into negotiations with the factory to reach an agreement."

"Early termination of the contract entitles the lender to compensation".

F

"The judge found in favour of Mr. Right and awarded him compensation to the amount of £10,000"

"Using a computer programme they factored in the costs of keeping the old machinery for the next three years"

H

"The judge handed down a suspended sentence"

"The land was handed down to him by his uncle, who died last year".

P

"The law provides that the penalty for a first offence can be up to 150 USD."

"She was accused of trying to pass off her logo for another company's".

"The Regulations provide that "traffic data" must be recorded and filed with the appropriate agency. "

S-Z

"The judge summed up the evidence presented by both sides before the jury made their decision"

"The Regulation sets forth the procedure for processing and fulfilment of orders"

"Articles 12 and 22 can unite the parties and contribute to advancing regional priorities within the framework set forth by the law."

"The judge can strike out the case if she decides that there are no reasonable grounds"

"The following article sets forth the basic terms of the contract."

"The judge weighed up the evidence for over an hour before handing down her verdict."

CHAPTER 10. MASTER BUSINESS IDIOMS & BUSINESS JARGON

"If you can't explain it simply, you don't understand it well enough."-

Albert Einstein

One of the greatest skills a business professional can have is the ability to translate technical or abstract concepts into simple, practical solutions.

When someone has specialist knowledge in an area, they often start to communicate using jargon expecting everyone to understand. Mix this with idioms and complex sentence structures and language, and it's no wonder we have miscommunications. Remember miscommunication costs time and money.

In some cases, your reader or listener might have the technical knowledge to have in-depth conversations about your product or service, but in most cases, even in business-to-business, what you need to focus on is solving problems! Jargon is usually unnecessary.

When trying to persuade people, translate your 'industry speak' to something that has a direct and meaningful message.

For example:

X will enable us to get the ball rolling on the specialist utilization of Y in order to provide a scaled solution to the challenges of Z.

↪

X will allow us to use Y (in order) to solve Z.

Summary:

- Become an authentic communicator
- Make your messages authentic and human by getting rid of business jargon.

- Use meaningful words to engage your audience.

Jargon	Meaning	The speaker or writer actually thinks
Value added	Improved	More attractive to clients or customers
Strategically engage departments	Communicate with departments	Try to find a way of improving participation from people in different departments. The current situation is not good.
Net-new business	New sources of revenue	New sources of money
The project is very difficult to **scale**	The project is very difficult to grow	The project is not going to make us much money
Shall we **circle back** on this?	Shall we talk about this another time?	I don't want to talk about this.
Our department currently does not have the **bandwidth** for this new initiative	Our department does not have the time or resources for this.	Our department cannot cope with another project, we have too much work as it is. If you want us to take on more projects, please give us more people and resources. Otherwise,

		don't bring any more 'initiatives' until we finish what we are currently working on please.
Will this new idea **move the needle**?	Will this new idea help us achieve our targets for a particular metric?	Will this move us forward in our objectives? Will it be useful in some way?

112 BUSINESS IDIOMS & COMMON TERMS WITH BETTER OPTIONS

A

1. "A-B testing"

"A-B testing" is a marketing term that describes when you test two very similar versions of a product or marketing campaign to see which one is superior.

2. "An 800-pound gorilla"

This is something that constitutes a threat. You could say "a force to be reckoned with". This would be more eloquent, because it's not as cliché.

3. "Actionable".

Something that is "actionable" is something you can take action on. It does not express whether the action would produce positive or negative results.

The following words have more impact and meaning than "actionable":

practical

useful

realistic

workable

4. "Action item".

There is no difference between "action item" and "action" or "task". The term is completely pointless and sub-communicates that you like to make easy things complicated, which is not a positive trait. Don't be the person who says "action item" please. Just say "action".

5. "An aha! moment"

A bit cliché.

Great options include

Revelation

Realization

Epiphany

insight

6. "ASAP"

It's much better to provide a specific time or date than to use ASAP. ASAP is rushed, dramatic and cliché. It is also unclear. For your lovely colleague Mary Higgins, "as soon as possible" might be next week, because she has several other tasks she's currently working on. Mary Higgins is not a mind-reader, so you need to help her by indicating an exact deadline.

7. "At the end of the day".

Very overused and carries very little meaning. It is essentially a space-filler.

Example:

~~At the end of the day,~~ it's extremely important to our long-term success.

8. "Awesome".

As someone who cannot stop saying this word, it's slightly hypocritical that I include it here. The problem with "awesome" is that it is so overused that it no longer expresses the full awesomeness of what you are trying to describe.

Other words you can use in business and professional settings are:

Exceptional

Marvellous

Magnificent

Superb

Outstanding

B

9. "Baked into".

it's accounted for

it's included

10. "Balls in the air"

This is vague and can be a bit distracting.

Present yourself as a confident and competent professional by saying what you mean.

Better options are

"I'm currently very busy with blah blah blah"

Or

"I'm currently working on several projects/tasks"

Or

"I have several projects/tasks underway".

11. "Bandwidth"

Like many cliché expressions and phrases, this one can be a little condescending. What the speaker/writer means here is "I/we don't have enough time/resources". But instead of saying it clearly, they are implying that not doing the task is part of their strategy somehow.

It's more respectful and eloquent to say *"we currently don't have the time/resources for X, Y, Z"*

12. "Bells and whistles".

This one is very common un the UK. It refers to attractive features or benefits added to a product or service to draw clients or customers. It always carries the connotation of "unnecessary", so avoid it when discussing your product or service.

Instead, you can say

"Features"

"Benefits"

13. A "bird's eye view", "a 10-20-30-40-50,000-foot view"

The expression comes from the idea of being in a high position so you can see everything that is happening. Taking a step back and looking at the situation without being distracted by being too heavily involved in any particular part of it. It tries to express an overall assessment based on impartial information.

The Message it Sends: The phrase is supposed to communicate authority, but it also asks for trust. This expression is so overused that it has lost its impact and therefore part of its meaning. It sub-communicates that objectivity comes with distance, which may or may not be true.

The speaker of this phrase is claiming that they can see more, because they have the data, or because they have a unique position or perspective.

It's often used in contexts in which staff are struggling while a manager or consultant is trying to convince them to trust him or her. In reality, the meaning would be expressed much more powerfully if you explained the situation or logical reasoning behind a decision.

13. "Bleeding edge", "cutting edge", "state-of-the-art".

These phrases are generally OK, but they don't carry much power because they are so generic and overused.

More specific ways of expressing the same meaning are:

"ground-breaking"

Or even

"unconventional"

or

"unorthodox"

14. "Boil the ocean."

This is office poetry for "waste time". It's much clearer and more eloquent to say "waste time".

15. "Brain surgery" and "rocket science".

"It's not rocket science!". This expression has been very overused and it's a bit of a joke. Outside of the office, it's often said jokingly or mockingly to someone who is struggling to understand or do something. For these reasons, it's much better to avoid it in professional settings. Instead, use a word with no connotations.

"It's relatively <u>simple</u>"

Or

"It's not <u>complicated</u>"

16. "Brick and mortar".

"Brick and mortar" can carry the connotation of *"traditional"*, or even *"old fashioned"* in some cases.

"Physical location" is a 100% neutral alternative to express the same thing.

17. "Bring to the table".

A more precise and clear way of expressing this is *"contribute"*.

18. To get "buy-in" or to get someone/people "on-board"

Both these expressions are the same as saying "get support".

It's much easier and more effective to say

"acceptance"

Or

"agreement"

Or

"support"

C

19. to "champion"

Better options are:

spearhead

support

defend

20. "Agent of change" or "change agent"

Slightly pompous. This expression gives the thing or person you are referring to almost God-like qualities.

21. "Check the box".

"Checking boxes" is a task you do because you have to. It's a formality that needs to be completed on paper. The implication of this expression is that it's unnecessary, so be careful when you use it.

22. We can "circle back" to that at the end of the meeting.

This just means that we can talk about the topic again at the end of the meeting.

23. "Circular file"

This is a joking way to say "bin" or "trash"

24. "Close the loop"

"I just wanted to close the loop on our emails regarding XYZ Ltd."

This is used to be polite when you need to get information from someone who is taking a bit longer than they should to answer your emails or calls.

24. "Competitive advantage".

This is just means that a company or product is very strong compared to its competitors. It's an advantage over the competition.

25. "Core competencies."

This means specialisms. Areas you or your company specialize in, or specific skills/areas that are extremely important to focus on.

26. "Corporate culture".

This is an overly complicated way of referring to a company's office environment and general atmosphere.

27. "Cross-training"

This is when a member of staff or department receive <u>extensive in-depth training</u> about another area of the business.

D

28. "Deck" or "Slide Deck"

This is a slide presentation (PowerPoint etc.)

29. "Deep dive".

In-depth analysis or examination.

"Deep dive" is very commonly used to the point that it has lost any power as a phrase.

Other options include:

Explore

Analyse

30. "Deliverable"

"Deliverable" means product or service that an agency delivers to the client. It's usually vague and unnecessary. It's much more personal and specific to name the product or work you will deliver to the client or that the agency will deliver to you.

31. "Disambiguate"

This is unnecessary and pompous in most cases. It's another word that overcomplicates. Whenever someone overcomplicates, it can come across as insecure or deceitful, so keep your communication open and honest by using less ridiculous options:

Make clear

Clarify

Simplify

Explain

32. "A disconnect"

This is a vague way of referring to a "difference of opinion", "disagreement" or "misunderstanding". If you say; "we had a disconnect", nobody will know what you are talking about, and if you say it enough times, not even *you* will know! So, unless you have a good reason for hiding the specific type of problem you had, be clear and honest:

We had a disagreement

We had a difference of opinion

We had a misunderstanding

33. "Disruptive"

"Disruptive" is another way of describing a product, service or company that changes the market in some way. It's best not to use it to describe your own company or its products, as it can seem disingenuous. Companies that are truly "disruptive" don't run around shouting about how "disruptive" they are.

34. "Drill down"

Examine

Look into

Look more closely at

Analyse

35. "Drop dead date"

Refers to a strict deadline specified in a contract or agreement. If this deadline is broken there will be serious consequences.

If you use this expression often, your audience will not take it seriously.

Instead, you can use:

Deadline

Due date

Cut off date

Target date

Time frame

36. To get your "ducks in a row".

To get organised.

This a harmless, fun expression. There is nothing really wrong with it, except that people who have never heard it before won't know what it means. You might want to avoid it in an international setting, where there are people from different parts of the world, as it could cause some confusion.

E

37. "Ecosystem".

An "ecosystem" can be sued to refer to software, where the user has continuous and in-depth interaction with the system. For example: Microsoft Windows.

Another use of the word "ecosystem" in business, is to refer to a network of products or services that the customer interacts with (buying and using). This is a useful way of referring to a related group of products or services.

38. "Empower"

"Empower" comes from the world of political activism. It is connected to rights, struggle, and conflict. It is better to talk about *giving* or *assigning responsibility*.

39. "Epic"

If everything is "epic", then nothing is truly "epic". This adjective is very extreme, and is casually overused in every-day conversation, so if you want to convey more meaning you can use:

Extraordinary

Practical

Applicable

Etc.

Anything that accurately describes what you are talking or writing about.

40. "Evangelist"

An "evangelist" is a brand fanatic who verges on total obsession, not a "loyal customer" or "casual user".

41. "Execute" and "Implement"

This is NOT another way of saying "do". "Implement" and "execute" mean that you will apply something in practice. If you mean "do", say "do".

F

42. It's time to "fish or cut bait".

It's time to make a decision!

"Fish or cut bait" is an informal expression that means "make a decision." There isn't really anything wrong with it, but avoid in international settings where people might have never heard it before.

43. "Frictionless"

Nothing worth discussing is ever 100% "frictionless" in business. Your audience are likely to know this subconsciously, so gain more credibility by saying:

the least amount of friction possible

or

minimal friction

44. "Functionality"

Instead of saying

multi-user interface functionality for A-B testing.

say

supports multiple users for A-B testing.

It's clear, meaningful, and easy to read.

G

45. "Game changer"

A "game changer" is something that changes everything, so it's important not to overuse this expression. Other, more specific options are:

important change (formal version: "significant shift")

fundamental change (formal version: "fundamental shift")

45. "Give time back"

If we close the JC Samuel account by Friday morning, we can finish early and "give everyone some time back".

The expression comes from the idea of not taking more time off people than you need to. It's saying, I realise this is time-consuming, so let's get it finished so we can get back to our main jobs or our private lives.

The Message it Sends: The expression is supposed to show goodwill, but if you deploy it in the wrong situation, it could create resentment or irritation.

To illustrate:

1. Jenny has just called a meeting and kept everyone in the room for 45 minutes providing information that could have been provided in a simple email.
2. She can see people are getting slightly tired and impatient, which makes her anxious.
3. To show she understands how they feel she says "Ok, if we can get through this last slide, we can finish this meeting early and give everyone some time back".
4. Some of the members of staff feel even more irritated now. Jenny has wasted 45 minutes of their time with something that could have been included in an email and is now telling them she is going to let them finish the meeting 10 minutes earlier than expected as if it was a gesture. If Jenny thought their time was so

precious, the real gesture would have been to write a clear email that they could read!

46. We are "good to go".

This is an informal way of saying "we are ready".

47. To take a "granular" look at something

This just means that you will examine something in detail.

Better options are:

Examine

Analyse

Look at in detail

Look at the details

48. "Guesstimate".

The word "guess" echoes in the audience's head here. Most of the time, it's best to avoid telling your listeners or readers that you're guessing.

Instead, you can say:

rough calculation

rough estimate

approximation

estimation

49. "Guru"

Do not describe yourself as a "guru", EVER!

If you want to describe someone else, you can use:

Expert

Leader

Authority

H

50. "Herding cats".

This phrase describes the act of managing a difficult group of people. It's an insult to the people you are referring to, so use with caution!

51. "Holistic" approach

All-encompassing

Complete

Comprehensive

52. "Human capital"

Very cold and impersonal way to refer to your people. Other options include:

Team

Staff

Employees

Workers

Workforce

I

53. "Incentivize"

This is to offer rewards in order to motivate staff. Most of the time it's better to talk about "motivating" staff, because that's essentially what we are trying to achieve.

54. "In light of the fact that".

A long, complicated way of saying *"because"*

55. "Innovative"

It's always better to specify *how* the product, service or company is "innovative", rather than simply throwing this overused adjective at your audience.

J

56. "Jump the shark."

This is a metaphor to express that a business, service, or product is declining. It is probably better to stay clear of metaphors and state exactly what you mean.

Example

~~"Product X has jumped the shark"~~

"Product X is past its prime"

Or

"Product X is in decline"

K

57. "Key takeaways"

Another way of saying:

"key points"

or

"most important points"

58. Killer app

This is an app with lots of potential for success. It's best to be specific in your description rather than use this expression.

59. "Knowledge transfer"

It doesn't get any worse than this. Just say *"teach"*.

L

60. "Laser focus."

Saying "laser focus" is like saying "extreme focus". It's usually unnecessary, and the expression is a little overused.

61. "Learnings".

This is not a word. "Learning" is not a noun that can be used instead of the word "lesson".

62. "Level playing field".

fair competition.

64. Level set

Once the department has been formed and the new office is up and running, we should call a department-wide meeting to "level set".

The expression comes from the idea of providing the same level of information to all parties. "Level-setting" means to ensure everyone involved in a project has the exact same information and expectations.

The Message it Sends: This can be a slightly confusing one, since many people use it wrongly. It sounds smart and professional, but it doesn't add much else, so beware.

63. "Leverage" (verb).

to use something to get what you want.

*We must **leverage** technology to advance the UK's higher education goals.*

The sentence above is OK, but by using the word "leverage", we are complicating a very simple concept.

It sounds less pretentious to say or write:

*We must **use** technology to advance the UK's higher education goals.*

64. Put "lipstick on a pig".

This is when you try to superficially cover up the negative qualities of something so that it looks better. This expression should be used with caution in international settings where it could cause confusion.

"Any attempt to redesign the product packaging would be like putting lipstick on a pig. The product has numerous quality issues that need to be resolved first."

65. "Low-hanging fruit".

A metaphor for "easily achievable options". As with all other metaphors, this one should be used with caution. It's often much more powerful to stay away from clichés and instead say exactly what you mean.

*"~~With the right strategy, lowering methane levels is~~ **a low-hanging fruit** ~~that can have a huge impact on greenhouse gas emissions.~~"*

*"With the right strategy, lowering methane levels is an **easily achievable objective** that can have a huge impact on greenhouse gas emissions."*

66. "Luddite".

Someone who opposes technological innovation for no good reason other than the fact that they don't like change.

M

67. "Magic bullet", "Magic solution", or "Magic remedy".

Something that will solve a problem without causing any negative side effects.

You can also use:

A cure-all

68. "Make hay while the sun shines".

To make the most of something.

Other options:

"Make the most of this opportunity"

69. "Methodology".

One of the most pretentious words in the English language. "Methodology" is so overused in business, that it has lost most of its meaning and impact. Instead, it's much more powerful to describe *processes* or *systems*.

70. "Mission-critical".

This is the perfect expression if you want to sound like a Special Forces soldier, or a secret agent. However, if you're interested in communicating clearly in business, just say:

critical

vital

essential

71. "Move the needle".

A metaphor to mean "improve as a business". It is better to either specify what results you are talking about, or simply talk about an "increase in sales", or an "increase in net profits" for example.

72. "My bad".

This expression makes it sound like you think the mistake was unimportant, or you want to present it as unimportant. It could lead to conflict or resentment if used in the wrong situation.

Better option:

"Sorry, I made a mistake"

N

73. as a "next step" we can

To be clearer and more direct, you can write:

"As a next step we can"

"Next, we can..."

74. Ninja.

Do not describe yourself as a "ninja", EVER!

If you want to describe someone else, you can use:

Expert

Leader

Authority

75. "One throat to choke".

This is an informal expression to describe the benefit of purchasing goods or services from only one provider. If you only use one provider, then when there is a problem, there is only "one throat to choke."

76. To be "on the same page".

To agree on how things should be done or handled. This expression is OK, but it's overused, so it's a bit diluted.

~~I just want to make sure we are on the same page.~~

It's easier to say:

I just want to make sure we agree.

77. "Open the books".

"Open the books" is when an organization or a team share private business information or projects with a possible investor or partner.

78. "Optimize".

This is a very common word in business.

Other options are:

Improve

fine-tune

enhance

79. to be "out of pocket".

Very common expression in the UK: to lose money from a business deal.

"We're out of pocket after the last shipment was delayed at customs."

This expression is less common outside of the UK, and many people may not have heard it before. It's usually best to specify:

"We lost money"

or

"We made a loss"

80. To think "outside the box".

To solve problems, in creative, original, and imaginative ways.

It's very over-used, and it signals to the listener or reader that you have not used any creativity in your choice of language. So "think outside the box" a little and use something else ⏺

Other options:

ingenuity

creativity

inventiveness

imagination

P

81. "Pain point"

This expression comes from marketing. It refers to a specific need that your ideal customer has. How can your product or service improve their lives and remove this "pain point" or *"problem""*?

Other options:

"problem"

"frustration"

"challenge"

82. "Paradigm shift".

This is not The Matrix.

It's easier to say:

"significant change"

83. To "pencil in".

To put someone or something on a schedule or a list, knowing that there may be changes later. Just like something written in pencil can be erased, this can be changed.

84. "Price point".

"Price points" are points on a scale of possible prices at which something can be sold. The term is often used when we try to predict changes in demand for a product which will result from different prices or "price points".

Every "price point" is a "price", so you can normally use "price" instead of "price point", even though they are not strictly the same thing.

85. To be "proactive".

Proactive is a little overused, and it has therefore lost some meaning. It's a word that is tossed into conversation and business writing so regularly that it has become bland and boring. A better option could be:

To "take the initiative"

86. "Push the envelope"

To go beyond normal limits or to try something seen as radical or dangerous. This expression is OK, but it really takes away from the message. A better option might be to specify the type of behaviour you are referring to.

John is a great executive, but he tends to push the envelope.

John is a great executive, but he tends to take unnecessary risks.

R

87. "Radio silence".

This is when a customer, client, or potential partner stops answering messages or calls. The expression comes from military. In a business context, the word "radio" does not add any extra meaning. It's far easier and more effective to say or write what you mean.

"Mr. Bloggs has stopped responding."

88. "Raise the bar".

This is a tired expression that means "to increase the level of what is expected".

Instead, you can say

"set higher standards"

"raise standards"

89. "Rationalization".

Cutbacks and structural changes within a business. It is much more effective to specify the changes to which you are referring. It can also earn you respect by not being vague and condescending.

90. "Reach out."

This expression is needlessly vague.

If you want to be vague because you don't know how you will contact the person, you can say *"contact"*

If you know how you will communicate with the person or group, then you should specify:

Call

Visit

Email

Etc.

91. "Reinvent the wheel".

"There's no need to reinvent the wheel!"

This expression describes the process of redesigning or changing something instead of using a tried and tested tool or method. If there is a highly effective method or tool you can use, then it doesn't make sense to invest time and effort into creating a new one.

92. "Resonate."

"His ideas on climate change really resonated with the audience."

This means that the audience was able to relate to his ideas on an emotional or logical level.

Other options:

"The audience really connected with his ideas on climate change."

"The audience was able to relate to his ideas on climate change."

"His ideas on climate change were really felt in the audience."

93. Right-sizing

This means 'downsizing', which involves cut-backs and usually lay-offs. The inclusion of the word "right" instead of "down" tries to make the change sound more legitimate and less alarming.

The Message it Sends: Saying "right-sizing" is supposed to eliminate some of the negative connotations of downsizing and express the need for the changes proposed, but it usually comes across as condescending and therefore disrespectful. If someone means downsizing, they should say downsizing.

93. "Rock star".

Do not describe yourself as a "rock star", EVER!

If you want to describe someone else, you can use:

Expert

Leader

Authority

S

94. "Secret sauce".

A company's "secret sauce" is their competitive advantage. What can you do that your competitor's can't do as well?

Secret sauce, makes something very important sound less important. It's making a joke about something crucial to your business.

Better choices are:

Competitive advantage

Unique advantage

Key advantage

95. "Sense of urgency".

If there is a real concern about something that needs to be done as quickly as possible, then you can use more authentic language than the clichéd "sense of urgency".

It is far more powerful to be specific about what you are doing:

We are working 12 hours a day on this at the moment.

We are putting all our focus on this at the moment.

Even

We are working round the clock on this at the moment.

Or you can describe your concern without the cliché:

We are extremely concerned about this.

96. Put/have "skin in the game".

When you are risking something you tend to be more motivated to achieve your goals. This is the meaning of this expression. It's a graphic way to describe this ownership concept, but it may not be understood by people who speak English as a second language. It's also a little informal for some contexts, so use with caution.

97. "Solutions".

In business, this is an overused and vague word that does nothing to express your message.

Instead of

Our software offers small business solutions.

Be a bit more specific and say

Our software simplifies accounting and tax for small businesses.

Or

Our software simplifies strategy and planning for small businesses.

98. "Soup to nuts".

Instead, use:

Full

Complete

All-inclusive

Exhaustive

Or

Comprehensive

99. "State of the art".

Avoid clichés if you are describing something related to your company.

Instead, describe it as

your newest product

or

the most advanced design

etc.

100. "Strike while the iron is hot."

To make the most of something.

Other options:

"Make the most of this opportunity"

101. "Synergy".

Synergy is when two or more things work together to have more effect than they have by themselves. Synergy is very real in business, but the word has been used wrongly so many times it has become diluted. A common mistake is to use it to "sell" a *collaboration*, or a *cooperation*. The rule is to only use "synergy" when you are talking about real synergy. If not, use a more appropriate word to convey your message.

T

102. "Table stakes".

Minimum requirements.

As with many expressions "table stakes" can cause confusion among people who have never heard it before, and it can dilute your message among those who know the meaning of the expression.

103. "Take strides".

When you say you have "taken strides".. the meaning is that you have improved a great deal. However, the connotation is that you were in a bad position initially and have improved a great deal since then. Because of the connotation, use this expression with caution.

104. Take a step back

Let's "take a step back".

It comes from the idea of physically taking a step back to get away from a physical confrontation. The meaning refers to a non-physical confrontation most of the time.

The Message it Sends: If used correctly, it's a little cliché, but it can help as a way of breaking the tension slightly before addressing the disagreement in a constructive way.

If the speaker simply throws the phrase out and changes the subject, it does not serve any purpose other than to annoy the listener. If it's used like this, it means "I don't like what you said, but let's not have a confrontation, even though I'm not prepared to talk about it." Regardless of how the speaker means it, this translates to "I do not respect you". This is an extremely unproductive way of using this expression.

104. "Take to the next level".

This means that you have improved a great deal. The connotation is that you were in a good position initially and have improved a great deal since then. Because of the connotation, use this expression with caution.

105. Thought leader

Do not describe yourself as a "thought leader", EVER!

If you want to describe someone else, you can use:

Expert

Leader

Authority

106. "Touch base"

Let's "touch base" again later this week.

The expression comes from baseball and it just means that we will have another meeting about the same topic later.

Instead of saying

let's meet later on this week and talk about this again.

we can save some words and be more detached by saying

Let's "touch base" again later this week.

The Message it Sends: It can sub-communicate that the relationship you have with the person is purely professional. It can communicate slight coldness or detachment.

This expression is needlessly vague.

If you want to be vague because you don't know how you will contact the person, you can say *"get in touch"* or *"get together"*.

If you know how you will communicate with the person or group, then you should specify:

Call

Visit

Email

Etc.

107. Get "traction".

To *"gather momentum"*, is a better option, as it describes the meaning better and isn't as formulaic.

U

108. "Utilize".

An over-complicated way of saying *"use"*

V

109. "Value-added".

It is meaningless if you say your product or service has "value-added" features or components. Focus instead on describing its benefits.

W

110. "White Paper"

A white paper is an official report, usually providing an authoritative guide to an industry or a market. It should not be used unless you are referring to this.

111. "With all due respect".

This is what people say when they are about to insult or disrespect somebody. Using this phrase before disrespect and insults, makes it even more painful for the receiver.

Z

112. Zero-sum game.

"Splitting the budget is a zero-sum game."

A "zero-sum game" is any occassion when one side can win only by making the other side lose. Many people don't know this expression, so use with caution.

BONUS CHAPTER 11. FREE BOOK: FINANCE & INVESTMENT TERMS EXPLAINED

Sign up to the FREE VIP List today to grab your FREE downloadable Digital Book ☺

I hope you have found this book useful. Thank you for reading.

https://www.idmbusinessenglish.com/free-ebook-investment-terms-explained

Other Business English Books in This Series by Marc Roche

<u>Business English Writing: Advanced Masterclass by Marc Roche</u>

Business Email: Write to Win

by Marc Roche

***Email Writing: Advanced* by**

Marc Roche

***Business Writing Skills Workbook: Master Business Grammar, Punctuation & Style* by Marc Roche**

The End & Special Thank You

If you enjoyed this book or found it helpful, I'd be very grateful if you'd post a short review on Amazon. Your support does make a difference, and I read all the reviews personally, so I can get your feedback and make this book even better.

If you did not enjoy this book, OR if you need any help finding the FREE templates, **please email us directly so that we can help!**

marc@idmbusinessenglish.com

Thanks for reading, and thanks again for your support!

Printed in Great Britain
by Amazon